TAGAKI 50
多書き

TAGAKI（多書き）とは、一言で言えば、「英語で自分を表現することを学ぶための、ボルダリング競技みたいなもの」です。その足場はメンタル面と英語面の2種類で、この足場を使って登って行き頂上を目指しましょう。このTAGAKIでは、考える→書く→伝えるを30トピック繰り返すことで、自分の意見を持ち、英語を書けるようになります。そうすると世界に飛び出して行けそうな自分を感じることができるでしょう。

TAGAKI 50 Contents もくじ

このワークブックの進め方		4

Topics		Categories	
1	◎Japan▸ **Albatrosses** (アホウドリ)	Living Things	6
2	⊕World▸ **Alpacas** (アルパカ)	Living Things	8
3	⊕World▸ **Beautiful Deserts** (美しい砂漠)	Nature	10
4	◎Japan▸ **Bonsai Trees** (盆栽)	Art	12
5	⊕World▸ **Dracula** (ドラキュラ)	History	14
6	⊕World▸ **Dragon Fruit** (ドラゴンフルーツ)	Food	16
7	◎Japan▸ **Edo Period** (江戸時代)	Culture	18
8	⊕World▸ **Gorillas** (ゴリラ)	Living Things	20
9	⊕World▸ **Honey** (ハチミツ)	Food	22
10	◎Japan▸ **Hot Spring Effects** (温泉の効能)	Nature	24
11	⊕World▸ **Jackfruit** (ジャックフルーツ)	Food	26
12	⊕World▸ **Judo** (柔道)	Sport	28
13	⊕World▸ **Kabaddi** (カバディ)	Sport	30
14	◎Japan▸ **Kamakura** (鎌倉)	Places	32
15	⊕World▸ **Knock on Wood** (木をコツコツたたく)	Culture	34
16	⊕World▸ **Machu Picchu** (マチュピチュ)	History	36
17	◎Japan▸ **Nobel Prize** (ノーベル賞)	Science	38
18	◎Japan▸ **Rain** (雨)	Nature	40
19	⊕World▸ **Reindeer** (トナカイ)	Living Things	42
20	◎Japan▸ **Snow Festival** (雪まつり)	Culture	44
21	⊕World▸ **Spaghetti** (スパゲッティ)	Food	46

22	⊕World▶ **Spreading Pollution**（広がる汚染）	Environment	48
23	⊕World▶ **Stonehenge**（ストーンヘンジ）	Mystery	50
24	⊕World▶ **Taekwondo**（テコンドー）	Sport	52
25	⊕World▶ **Tooth Fairy**（歯の妖精）	Culture	54
26	⊙Japan▶ **Volcanoes**（火山）	Nature	56
27	⊕World▶ **Watching Sport**（スポーツ観戦）	Sport	58
28	⊕World▶ **Weightlessness**（無重力）	Science	60
29	⊕World▶ **Whale Songs**（クジラの歌）	Living Things	62
30	⊕World▶ **Yetis**（イエティ）	Mystery	64

進度表 終わったトピックの番号に印をつけていきましょう！

TAGAKI 50 をはじめよう

トピックのテーマについて検索し、その結果を英文に反映し、独自性を出していくことにチャレンジしましょう。テーマについて検索をした際、みんなの意見が同じ内容になってしまうのではないかと思うかもしれませんが、そんなはずはありません。どうしてかというと、世の中にはたくさんの情報があふれているということと、学習者それぞれの意見が同じではないからです。

進め方

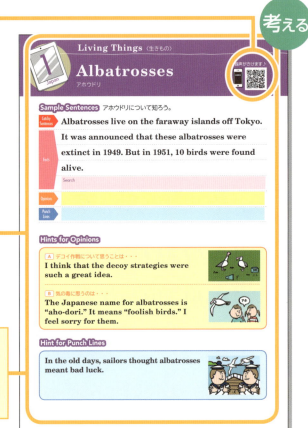

1人でTAGAKIを学ぶ人へ
単独の良さをいかし、自由に自分のペースでStep1〜5を進んでください。自分で自分の進歩を見届け、それぞれの目的や目標、例えば入試や検定試験、会議やプレゼンなどのために書く力を付けてください。

TAGAKI 50 目標

メンタル	自分の意見を述べ、「おち」も自分で考える

自分が何を考えているかは無意識な部分も多く、それを引き出す練習が必要です。ヒントを参考に自分の意見をひねり出してください。そしてパンチラインで自分の独自性を出しましょう。

英語	検索した結果を英文に反映し、50語前後の英文を書く

まず、日本語で検索し、おおよその背景知識を得てから英語版で検索を見て、自分が必要な単語やフレーズを拾い英文をまとめましょう。

検索元や検索内容、キーワードなどを書き留めておきましょう！

書く 7～10分で書きましょう。

Step 3 Writing

Sample Sentences の Catchy Sentences と Facts のリード文を書き写し、自分が検索した結果でおもしろかった内容を選び、Facts に書き加えましょう。
Hints for Opinions を参考にして Opinions に自分の意見を書きましょう。
Hint for Punch Lines を参考に、Punch Lines に自分のオリジナルのパンチラインを書きましょう。

Step 4 Writing

Writing Time ❶ で書いた文を見ないで、もう一度書きましょう。

伝える

Step 5 Speaking

Writing Time ❷ で書いた文を覚えて声に出して言いましょう。

ペアやグループでTAGAKIを学ぶ人へ	Step1～5を進めた後、友達や家族、先生に向けて発表したり、他の人の発表を聞いて、英語または日本語でディスカッションしたりして、4技能の学習へ発展してください。書いたものは見ないで発表しましょう。

Living Things 〈生きもの〉

Albatrosses
アホウドリ

音声がきけます♪

Sample Sentences アホウドリについて知ろう。

Catchy Sentences: Albatrosses live on the faraway islands off Tokyo.

Facts: It was announced that these albatrosses were extinct in 1949. But in 1951, 10 birds were found alive.

Opinions:

Punch Lines:

Hints for Opinions

A　デコイ作戦について思うことは・・・
I think that the decoy strategies were such a great idea.

B　気の毒に思うのは・・・
The Japanese name for albatrosses is "aho-dori." It means "foolish birds." I feel sorry for them.

Hint for Punch Lines

In the old days, sailors thought albatrosses meant bad luck.

アホウドリについて調べよう。

Writing Time

1 自分で Facts を調べて書き加えよう。 Opinions Punch Lines を考えて全文を書こう。

Catchy Sentences

Facts

Opinions

Punch Lines

2 上で書いた文を見ないで書いて、見ないで言おう。

Catchy Sentences

Facts

Opinions

Punch Lines

Living Things 〈生きもの〉

Alpacas
アルパカ

音声がきけます♪

Sample Sentences アルパカについて知ろう。

Catchy Sentences
Alpacas are useful animals for people, especially in the Andes in South America.

Facts
I've learned that the fleece of alpacas is used for ponchos.

Search

Opinions

Punch Lines

Hints for Opinions

A びっくりしたことは・・・
It's amazing that some people have alpacas as pets.

B かわいいと思うことは・・・
I think that alpacas look cute because their eyelashes are long. They seem to smile for you, too.

Hint for Punch Lines

They should hold beauty competitions to see which alpaca is cutest!

TAGAKI 50

アルパカについて調べよう。

Writing Time

1 自分で Facts を調べて書き加えよう。 Opinions Punch Lines を考えて全文を書こう。

- Catchy Sentences
- Facts
- Opinions
- Punch Lines

2 上で書いた文を見ないで書いて、見ないで言おう。

- Catchy Sentences
- Facts
- Opinions
- Punch Lines

9

Nature 〈自然〉

Beautiful Deserts
美しい砂漠

音声がきけます♪

Sample Sentences 砂漠の美しさを知ろう。

Catchy Sentences: Deserts are beautiful. Some of them look like hills, rivers, and even oceans.

Facts: I found out that deserts change their shapes because of strong sandstorms.

Search

Opinions:

Punch Lines:

Hints for Opinions

A 理解したことは・・・

I understand that deserts attract many photographers and artists because of their beauty.

B 驚いたことは・・・

It's surprising that some beautiful flowers bloom in deserts.

Hint for Punch Lines

By the way, my mouth is as dry as a desert.

TAGAKI 50

砂漠の美しさについて調べよう。

Writing Time

1 自分で Facts を調べて書き加えよう。 Opinions Punch Lines を考えて全文を書こう。

Catchy Sentences

Facts

Opinions

Punch Lines

2 上で書いた文を見ないで書いて、見ないで言おう。

Catchy Sentences

Facts

Opinions

Punch Lines

Art 〈芸術〉

Bonsai Trees
盆栽

音声がきけます♪

Sample Sentences 盆栽の世界を知ろう。

Catchy Sentences: Bonsai trees are amazing! They're often called "living art."

Facts: I didn't know that bonsai trees are becoming more and more popular in many foreign countries.

Search

Opinions:

Punch Lines:

Hints for Opinions

A 信じがたいことは・・・
It's unbelievable that some of them have tiny real fruit such as persimmons and apples.

B 誇りに思うことは・・・
I'm proud that bonsai trees are a wonderful part of Japanese tradition.

Hint for Punch Lines

Wouldn't it be fun if we could grow bonsai pets? I could have a real mini-elephant on my hand!

TAGAKI 50

盆栽(ぼんさい)の世界について調べよう。

Writing Time

1 自分で Facts を調べて書き加えよう。 Opinions Punch Lines を考えて全文を書こう。

Catchy Sentences

Facts

Opinions

Punch Lines

2 上で書いた文を見ないで書いて、見ないで言おう。

Catchy Sentences

Facts

Opinions

Punch Lines

13

History 〈歴史〉

Dracula
ドラキュラ

音声がきけます♪

Sample Sentences ドラキュラの真実を知ろう。

Catchy Sentences	Dracula's full name is Vlad Dracula. He was born on November 10th, 1431, in Romania.
Facts	I found out that Dracula was a powerful king. Even today, he's a hero in his country.
	Search
Opinions	
Punch Lines	

Hints for Opinions

A 知ってうれしいことは・・・
I'm glad to know that Dracula as a vampire became popular because of the novel written by Bram Stoker, from Ireland.

B 自分がしたいことは・・・
I want to read some books to find out the true history.

Hint for Punch Lines

I wonder if Vlad Dracula had any friends.

14

TAGAKI 50

ドラキュラの真実について調べよう。

Writing Time

1 自分で Facts を調べて書き加えよう。 Opinions Punch Lines を考えて全文を書こう。

- Catchy Sentences
- Facts
- Opinions
- Punch Lines

2 上で書いた文を見ないで書いて、見ないで言おう。

- Catchy Sentences
- Facts
- Opinions
- Punch Lines

15

Food 〈食べもの〉

Dragon Fruit
ドラゴンフルーツ

音声がきけます♪

Sample Sentences ドラゴンフルーツについて知ろう。

Catchy Sentences: Dragon fruit is colorful. Some can be pink, yellow, or red.

Facts: Dragon fruit is grown in South America, Southeast Asia, Australia, and other places.

Search

Opinions

Punch Lines

Hints for Opinions

A おもしろいことは・・・

It's interesting that the outside and inside of dragon fruit are very different.

B 自分がするべきことは・・・

I should eat more dragon fruit because now I know it's nutritious. Dragon fruit has polyphenols, dietary fiber, and vitamins B1, B2, C, and so on.

Hint for Punch Lines

I think dragon fruit looks much prettier than it tastes.

TAGAKI 50

ドラゴンフルーツについて調べよう。

Writing Time

1 自分で Facts を調べて書き加えよう。 Opinions Punch Lines を考えて全文を書こう。

- Catchy Sentences
- Facts
- Opinions
- Punch Lines

2 上で書いた文を見ないで書いて、見ないで言おう。

- Catchy Sentences
- Facts
- Opinions
- Punch Lines

Culture 〈文化〉

Edo Period
江戸時代

音声がきけます♪

Sample Sentences 江戸時代の文化レベルの高さについて知ろう。

Catchy Sentences: Many people believe that the people of the Edo period enjoyed an advanced culture.

Facts: People enjoyed such cultural performances as sumo, rakugo (comic stories), and kabuki.

Search

Opinions:

Punch Lines:

Hints for Opinions

A 自分が知りたいことは・・・
I want to know more about Matsuo Basho (1644-1694) who wrote haiku that many people can recite even today.

B 偉大(いだい)なことは・・・
It's great that Katsushika Hokusai (1760-1849) produced his world famous drawings.

Hint for Punch Lines

Basho's most famous haiku reads: "An ancient pond / a frog jumps in / the splash of water." People all over the world know Hokusai's print "The Great Wave off Kanagawa."

TAGAKI 50

江戸時代の文化レベルの高さについて調べよう。

Writing Time

1 自分で Facts を調べて書き加えよう。 Opinions Punch Lines を考えて全文を書こう。

Catchy Sentences

Facts

Opinions

Punch Lines

2 上で書いた文を見ないで書いて、見ないで言おう。

Catchy Sentences

Facts

Opinions

Punch Lines

Living Things 〈生きもの〉

Gorillas
ゴリラ

音声がきけます♪

Sample Sentences　ゴリラの知能とコミュニケーション力について知ろう。

Catchy Sentences: Gorillas are very smart and good at communication.

Facts: I've learned that gorillas carefully look at the faces of other gorillas for communication.

Search

Opinions:

Punch Lines:

Hints for Opinions

A 驚いたことは・・・
It's surprising that the famous gorilla named Koko learned a large number of hand signs.

B 聞いた話によると・・・
I've heard that gorillas are peace lovers. I wonder if it's true that they don't fight with other species, for example, chimpanzees.

Hint for Punch Lines

I wish I was as strong as a gorilla, but also as gentle.

Food 〈食べもの〉

Honey
ハチミツ

音声がきけます♪

Sample Sentences ハチミツの不思議について知ろう。

 Catchy Sentences: Honeybees visit flowers 200 times to produce one teaspoonful of honey!

 Facts: I didn't know that honey was already eaten by the Egyptians around 1500 B.C.

Search

Opinions:

Punch Lines:

Hints for Opinions

A 信じられないことは・・・
I can't believe that about 20,000 honeybees work together to produce honey in one colony (box).

B 知って良かったことは・・・
It's good to know that honey is good for us because it has vitamins and minerals in it.

Hint for Punch Lines

Bees are known as hard workers. That's why there's the expression "as busy as a bee."

Nature 〈自然〉

Hot Spring Effects
温泉の効能

音声がきけます♪

Sample Sentences 温泉の効能について知ろう。

Catchy Sentences: People think some hot springs can heal physical problems such as knee pain, backache, and stiff shoulders.

Facts: Many samurai used hot springs to heal their wounds.

Search

Opinions:

Punch Lines:

Hints for Opinions

A 信じていることは・・・
I believe that the biggest effect of hot springs is to make people feel relaxed.

B ニホンザルでさえ・・・
Even Japanese monkeys enjoy hot springs. Maybe they know the effects.

Hint for Punch Lines

I always fall asleep in hot springs just like the monkeys!

24

Food 〈食べもの〉

Jackfruit
ジャックフルーツ

音声がきけます♪

Sample Sentences ジャックフルーツについて知ろう。

Catchy Sentences: Jackfruit is the biggest fruit in the world. Some can be as long as 50-90 centimeters and weigh as much as 40-50 kilograms.

Facts: Some people say jackfruit is the most delicious fruit in the world.

Search

Opinions

Punch Lines

Hints for Opinions

A 想像できなかったことは・・・
I couldn't imagine that the inside of a jackfruit looks like grapes.

B 信じられないことは・・・
I can't believe that it grows on a tree.

Hint for Punch Lines

If you ate a whole jackfruit, you would surely burst!

Sport 〈スポーツ〉

Judo
柔道（じゅうどう）

音声がきけます♪

Sample Sentences 柔道（じゅうどう）は国際的なスポーツだということを知ろう。

Catchy Sentences: Judo is an international sport. It became one of the Olympic sports in 1964.

Facts: Judo is popular in countries such as France, Mongolia, and Russia.

Search

Opinions

Punch Lines

Hints for Opinions

A びっくりしたことは・・・
It's amazing that even very young children do judo in France.

B 理解したことは・・・
I understand that judo is popular in many countries, because people learn courtesy and respect.

Hint for Punch Lines

Q: What color will you be if you're bad at judo?
A: Black and blue! (bruises)

28

TAGAKI 50

柔道は国際的なスポーツだということについて調べよう。

Writing Time

1 自分で ▶Facts▶ を調べて書き加えよう。 ▶Opinions▶ ▶Punch Lines▶ を考えて全文を書こう。

Catchy Sentences

Facts

Opinions

Punch Lines

2 上で書いた文を見ないで書いて、見ないで言おう。

Catchy Sentences

Facts

Opinions

Punch Lines

29

Sport 〈スポーツ〉

Kabaddi
カバディ

音声がきけます♪

Sample Sentences　カバディというスポーツを知ろう。

Catchy Sentences: Kabaddi is a unique sport! It's popular in such countries as Bangladesh, India, and Pakistan.

Facts: I've learned that kabaddi comes from an old hunting style without weapons.

Search

Opinions

Punch Lines

Hints for Opinions

[A] おもしろいことは・・・
It's interesting that the players keep saying "kabaddi" in a quiet voice within one breath.

[B] 自分がしたいことは・・・
I want to play it once to understand the rules.

Hint for Punch Lines

It's really fun to watch, but I don't understand the rules!

TAGAKI 50

カバディというスポーツについて調べよう。

Writing Time

1 自分で Facts を調べて書き加えよう。 Opinions Punch Lines を考えて全文を書こう。

- Catchy Sentences
- Facts
- Opinions
- Punch Lines

2 上で書いた文を見ないで書いて、見ないで言おう。

- Catchy Sentences
- Facts
- Opinions
- Punch Lines

Places 〈場所〉

Kamakura
鎌倉

音声がきけます♪

Sample Sentences 鎌倉の魅力について知ろう。

Catchy Sentences
Kamakura was the ancient capital of the Kamakura period (around 1185-1333).

Facts
The Great Buddha of Kamakura has been sitting there for over 750 years.

Search

Opinions

Punch Lines

Hints for Opinions

A 楽しそうなことは・・・
A trip to Kamakura by Enoshima Electric Railway will be great fun.

B たくさんのセレブが住む理由は・・・
A lot of celebrities have lived in this city. I think it's because they can enjoy history, nature, and good food.

Hint for Punch Lines

I'd like to go to Kamakura because it's beautiful, but I also might see a TV celebrity I like!

Culture 〈文化〉

Knock on Wood
木をコツコツたたく

Sample Sentences 木をコツコツたたくという迷信(めいしん)を知ろう。

Catchy Sentences: One day, a friend of mine said, "I haven't been sick this year. Knock on wood!"

Facts: If you knock on wood, you can keep good things going and avoid bad things.

Search

Opinions:

Punch Lines:

Hints for Opinions

A 知って良かったことは・・・
It's good to know that some people say "Touch wood!"

B なぜだろうと思うのは・・・
I wonder why Western people believe wood has some power.

Hint for Punch Lines

"Knock on wood! My soccer team will win this weekend."

34

TAGAKI 50

木をコツコツたたくという迷信について調べよう。

Writing Time

1 自分で Facts を調べて書き加えよう。 Opinions Punch Lines を考えて全文を書こう。

Catchy Sentences

Facts

Opinions

Punch Lines

2 上で書いた文を見ないで書いて、見ないで言おう。

Catchy Sentences

Facts

Opinions

Punch Lines

35

History 〈歴史〉

Machu Picchu
マチュピチュ

音声がきけます♪

Sample Sentences マチュピチュの不思議について知ろう。

Catchy Sentences: The Inca Empire built Machu Picchu 2,430 meters above sea level. Why?

Facts: The Inca people wanted to live in a safe place.
Search

Opinions:

Punch Lines:

Hints for Opinions

A　おもしろいことは・・・
It's interesting that Cusco, the capital city of the Inca Empire, is 1,000 meters higher than Machu Picchu.

B　残念だったのは・・・
It was too bad that the Incas didn't have a writing system.

Hint for Punch Lines

I wish I could eat Inca potatoes.

TAGAKI 50

マチュピチュの不思議について調べよう。

Writing Time

1 自分で `Facts` を調べて書き加えよう。 `Opinions` `Punch Lines` を考えて全文を書こう。

Catchy Sentences

Facts

Opinions

Punch Lines

2 上で書いた文を見ないで書いて、見ないで言おう。

Catchy Sentences

Facts

Opinions

Punch Lines

37

Science 〈科学〉

Nobel Prize
ノーベル賞

音声がきけます♪

Sample Sentences 日本人科学者のノーベル賞受賞について知ろう。

Catchy Sentences
Twenty-three Nobel Prizes have been awarded to Japanese people, as of 2017.

Facts
The award ceremony is held on December 10th, the anniversary of Alfred Nobel's death.

Search

Opinions

Punch Lines

Hints for Opinions

A なぜだろうと思うのは・・・
I wonder why Japanese scientists' strong areas are physics, chemistry, physiology, and medicine.

B 誇りに思うことは・・・
I'm proud of our scientists, although I'm not good at science.

Hint for Punch Lines

If there was a Nobel Prize for telling bad jokes, or not doing my homework, I would have won it.

TAGAKI 50

日本人科学者のノーベル賞受賞について調べよう。

Writing Time

1 自分で Facts を調べて書き加えよう。 Opinions Punch Lines を考えて全文を書こう。

- Catchy Sentences
- Facts
- Opinions
- Punch Lines

2 上で書いた文を見ないで書いて、見ないで言おう。

- Catchy Sentences
- Facts
- Opinions
- Punch Lines

Nature 〈自然〉

Rain
雨

音声がきけます♪

Sample Sentences 日本の雨について知ろう。

Catchy Sentences: It rains a lot in Japan. We get twice as much rain as the world's average.

Facts: I learned that it rained the most in Kochi Prefecture in 2017.

Search

Opinions:

Punch Lines:

Hints for Opinions

[A] 魅力的（みりょくてき）なのは・・・
It's fascinating that the Japanese language has many expressions for rain.

[B] 確信していることは・・・
I'm sure that all the rain makes Japan a very green country.

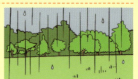

Hint for Punch Lines

I love the words of Kenji Miyazawa's poem: "I will not give in to the rain …"

TAGAKI 50

日本の雨について調べよう。

Writing Time

1 自分で Facts を調べて書き加えよう。 Opinions Punch Lines を考えて全文を書こう。

- Catchy Sentences
- Facts
- Opinions
- Punch Lines

2 上で書いた文を見ないで書いて、見ないで言おう。

- Catchy Sentences
- Facts
- Opinions
- Punch Lines

41

Living Things 〈生きもの〉

Reindeer
トナカイ

音声がきけます♪

Sample Sentences　トナカイの真実を知ろう。

Catchy Sentences: Reindeer are useful animals because of their milk, fur, horns, and meat.

Facts: Reindeer live mainly in Finland, Norway, Canada, Russia, and so on.

Search

Opinions:

Punch Lines:

Hints for Opinions

A　驚いたことは・・・
It's surprising that both male and female reindeer have huge antlers (horns).

B　移動する数は・・・
The migrating Siberian tundra reindeer in Russia sometimes number from 10,000 to 500,000.

Hint for Punch Lines

I think that the person who connected reindeer with Santa Claus was a genius.

42

TAGAKI 50

トナカイの真実について調べよう。

Writing Time

1 自分で Facts を調べて書き加えよう。 Opinions Punch Lines を考えて全文を書こう。

Catchy Sentences

Facts

Opinions

Punch Lines

2 上で書いた文を見ないで書いて、見ないで言おう。

Catchy Sentences

Facts

Opinions

Punch Lines

Culture 〈文化〉

Snow Festival
雪まつり

音声がきけます♪

Sample Sentences さっぽろ雪まつりについて知ろう。

Catchy Sentences: The Snow Festival in Sapporo is a huge winter festival.

Facts: A group of junior and senior high school students made the first snow sculptures in 1950.

Search

Opinions

Punch Lines

Hints for Opinions

[A] 魅力的なのは・・・
It's fascinating that some works are huge, but have finely made details.

[B] 素晴らしいことは・・・
It's great that this festival attracts more than two million (2,000,000) visitors every year.

Hint for Punch Lines

I know it's strange, but I like to eat ice cream while I look at the snow sculptures.

Food 〈食べもの〉

Spaghetti
スパゲッティ

音声がきけます♪

Sample Sentences スパゲッティの起源を知ろう。

Catchy Sentences: Some people say an Italian explorer Marco Polo brought spaghetti back from China in 1295.

Facts: It's commonly believed that Naples in Italy is the birthplace of spaghetti.

Search

Opinions

Punch Lines

Hints for Opinions

A 言われていることは・・・
It's said that spaghetti making machines were invented in the 19th century. I'd like to make my own spaghetti with those machines.

B 無理だと思うことは・・・
I don't think it's possible to find out the true origin of spaghetti.

Hint for Punch Lines

It doesn't matter where spaghetti or noodles were invented, I love them all!

TAGAKI 50

スパゲッティの起源について調べよう。

Writing Time

1 自分で Facts を調べて書き加えよう。 Opinions Punch Lines を考えて全文を書こう。

Catchy Sentences

Facts

Opinions

Punch Lines

2 上で書いた文を見ないで書いて、見ないで言おう。

Catchy Sentences

Facts

Opinions

Punch Lines

47

22 Environment 〈環境〉

Spreading Pollution
広がる汚染

音声がきけます♪

Sample Sentences PM2.5と黄砂について知ろう。

Catchy Sentences	Do you know anything about yellow sand and PM2.5?
Facts	Yellow sand is carried on high winds from the Gobi and Taklamakan Deserts.
	Search
Opinions	
Punch Lines	

Hints for Opinions

A 怖いことは・・・

It's scary that the particles of PM2.5 are as small as 1/30 (one-thirtieth) of a hair and can enter our lungs easily.

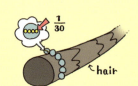

B 私たちがするべきことは・・・

We should be more conscious of air pollution problems.

Hint for Punch Lines

We all need to stop polluting the air we breathe!

Mystery 〈ミステリー〉

Stonehenge
ストーンヘンジ

音声がきけます♪

Sample Sentences ストーンヘンジのなぞを知ろう。

Catchy Sentences: Nobody knows how Stonehenge was made, or what for.

Facts: Some people say that it was used for a space observatory or an altar.

Search

Opinions:

Punch Lines:

Hints for Opinions

A 信じがたいことは・・・
It's unbelievable that even though each stone can weigh up to 50 tons, they don't fall.

B 自分がする必要があることは・・・
I need to go to Stonehenge to check if it's a power spot.

Hint for Punch Lines

Maybe I can use the power of Stonehenge to save the environment!

ストーンヘンジのなぞについて調べよう。

Writing Time

1 自分で Facts を調べて書き加えよう。 Opinions Punch Lines を考えて全文を書こう。

Catchy
Sentences

Facts

Opinions

Punch
Lines

2 上で書いた文を見ないで書いて、見ないで言おう。

Catchy
Sentences

Facts

Opinions

Punch
Lines

24 World

Sport 〈スポーツ〉

Taekwondo
テコンドー

音声がきけます♪

Sample Sentences テコンドーというスポーツを知ろう。

Catchy Sentences: Taekwondo originally comes from Korea. It's one of the Olympic sports.

Facts: Data shows that 70,000,000 (seventy million) people in 207 countries and regions do taekwondo.

Search

Opinions

Punch Lines

Hints for Opinions

A わかったことは・・・

Now I know that "tae" means "kick," "kwon" means "fist," and "do" means "way," the same as in judo, kendo, and aikido.

B 魅力的(みりょくてき)なのは・・・

It's fascinating how high they can kick and how quickly they can punch.

Hint for Punch Lines

Donkeys can kick very hard. It would be very scary if donkeys could do taekwondo.

TAGAKI 50

テコンドーというスポーツについて調べよう。

Writing Time

1 自分で Facts を調べて書き加えよう。 Opinions Punch Lines を考えて全文を書こう。

Catchy Sentences

Facts

Opinions

Punch Lines

2 上で書いた文を見ないで書いて、見ないで言おう。

Catchy Sentences

Facts

Opinions

Punch Lines

Culture 〈文化〉

Tooth Fairy
歯の妖精

音声がきけます♪

Sample Sentences 歯の妖精という迷信を知ろう。

Catchy Sentences
When children lose a baby tooth, what do they do?

Facts
In some countries, the tooth fairy comes during the night, takes the baby tooth, and leaves a coin under the pillow.

Search

Opinions

Punch Lines

Hints for Opinions

A 確信していることは・・・

I'm sure that the tooth fairy makes children feel better when they lose their teeth.

B 自分がしたかったことは・・・

I wanted to wait for the tooth fairy to come.

Hint for Punch Lines

I wonder what the tooth fairy does with all the teeth. There must be a lot!

54

歯の妖精という迷信について調べよう。

Writing Time

1 自分で Facts を調べて書き加えよう。 Opinions Punch Lines を考えて全文を書こう。

Catchy Sentences

Facts

Opinions

Punch Lines

2 上で書いた文を見ないで書いて、見ないで言おう。

Catchy Sentences

Facts

Opinions

Punch Lines

Nature 〈自然〉

Volcanoes
火山

音声がきけます♪

Sample Sentences 火山の恐怖と恩恵について知ろう。

Catchy Sentences: Many Japanese mountains are active volcanoes.

Facts: The most recent data shows that the number of active volcanoes is 111.

Search

Opinions:

Punch Lines:

Hints for Opinions

A 残念なことは・・・
I feel bad that some mountain climbers and hikers are sometimes affected by volcanic eruptions.

B 自分がなるほどと思うことは・・・
It makes sense to me that people in the Edo period called volcanoes "hell" and hot springs "paradise."

Hint for Punch Lines

My dad has a volcanic eruption if we talk while he's watching news on TV.

TAGAKI 50

火山の恐怖と恩恵について調べよう。

Writing Time

1 自分で `Facts` を調べて書き加えよう。 `Opinions` `Punch Lines` を考えて全文を書こう。

Catchy Sentences	
Facts	
Opinions	
Punch Lines	

2 上で書いた文を見ないで書いて、見ないで言おう。

Catchy Sentences	
Facts	
Opinions	
Punch Lines	

57

Sport 〈スポーツ〉

Watching Sport
スポーツ観戦

音声がきけます♪

Sample Sentences スポーツ観戦について知ろう。

Catchy Sentences: Three billion five hundred million (3,500,000,000) supporters watch soccer (football) games every year.

Facts: Data from one ranking shows that the top five most popular sports in the world are soccer, basketball, cricket, golf, and tennis.

Search

Opinions

Punch Lines

Hints for Opinions

A そのほか人気のスポーツは・・・
Other popular sports are ice hockey, volleyball, rugby, boxing, and baseball.

B 信じていることは・・・
I believe that watching sport is an important part of modern human life.

Hint for Punch Lines

Sport is what we have instead of war. Let's have more sport and less war!

TAGAKI 50

スポーツ観戦について調べよう。

Writing Time

1 自分で Facts を調べて書き加えよう。 Opinions Punch Lines を考えて全文を書こう。

Catchy Sentences

Facts

Opinions

Punch Lines

2 上で書いた文を見ないで書いて、見ないで言おう。

Catchy Sentences

Facts

Opinions

Punch Lines

Science 〈科学〉

Weightlessness
無重力

Sample Sentences 無重力について知ろう。

Catchy Sentences: Do you want to experience weightlessness?

Facts: If you want to become an astronaut, you have to go through training to endure up to nine gees (9 g).

Search

Opinions

Punch Lines

Hints for Opinions

A 知って良かったことは…
It's good to know that you can have an experience of weightlessness in a small jet based at Nagoya Airport.

B 怖いことは…
It's scary when your body feels pressed at two gees (2 g).

Hint for Punch Lines

The problem is your body doesn't know which way is up and which way is down.

Living Things 〈生きもの〉

Whale Songs
クジラの歌

音声がきけます♪

Sample Sentences クジラの歌について知ろう。

Catchy Sentences: Humpback whales sing. Their songs sound like squeaks or whistles.

Facts: It's well known that their songs are used to express love or to communicate with each other.

Search

Opinions

Punch Lines

Hints for Opinions

A 驚いたことは・・・

It's surprising that their songs can continue from several minutes to half an hour.

B なぜだろうと思うのは・・・

I wonder why their songs can be heard thousands of kilometers away. For example, they can be heard from Japan to Hawaii.

Hint for Punch Lines

It must be hard for whales to keep secrets if all the other whales can hear them thousands of kilometers away!

Mystery 〈ミステリー〉

Yetis
イエティ

音声がきけます♪

Sample Sentences イエティの真実を知ろう。

Catchy Sentences: People have been afraid of Yetis for a long time in the mountains of Tibet and Nepal.

Facts: It's historic that the recent research using DNA proved they were huge bears!

Search

Opinions

Punch Lines

Hints for Opinions

A 理解したことは・・・
I understand why some villagers believed Yetis were three meters tall. The villagers were just scared.

B 印象的なことは・・・
The modern research technologies are impressive.

Hint for Punch Lines

Bears sound less scary than Yetis, but I don't want to meet either when I'm in Tibet or Nepal.

コードを読み取れない方や音声をダウンロードしたい方は、右のQRコードまたは
以下のURLより、アクセスしてください。
https://www.mpi-j.co.jp/contents/shop/mpi/contents/digital/tagaki50.html

TAGAKI®50

発　行　日	●	2018年10月11日　初版第１刷　　2023年１月20日　第７刷
		2023年３月20日　　２版第１刷
執　　　　筆	●	松香洋子
執 筆 協 力	●	近藤理恵子
英 文 校 正	●	Glenn McDougall
編　　　　集	●	株式会社カルチャー・プロ
イ ラ ス ト	●	鹿野理恵子　メイ ボランチ
本文デザイン	●	DB Works
本 文 組 版	●	株式会社内外プロセス
録 音・編 集	●	一般財団法人英語教育協議会（ELEC）
ナレーション	●	Erica Williams　Jon Mudryj　Julia Yermakov
写 真 提 供	●	The Gorilla Foundation/AFP/WAA　AP　ロイター　アフロ
協　　　　力	●	赤松由梨　粕谷みゆき　貞野浩子　野中美恵　宮下いづみ　山内由紀子
印　　　　刷	●	シナノ印刷株式会社
発　　　　行	●	株式会社mpi松香フォニックス
		〒151-0053
		東京都渋谷区代々木2-16-2 第二甲田ビル 2F
		fax:03-5302-1652
		URL:https://www.mpi-j.co.jp

不許複製 All rights reserved.
©2018 mpi Matsuka Phonics inc.
ISBN 978-4-89643-749-2

＊本書で取り扱っている内容は、2017年までの情報をもとに作成しています。
＊QRコードは(株)デンソーウェーブの登録商標です。